Chapter 1: Introduction

Drug sales forecasting is an essential aspect of pharmaceutical companies' operations. The sales forecast helps the company plan for production, marketing, and distribution of their drugs. Sales forecasting also helps in financial planning and budgeting. Accurate sales forecasting can lead to cost savings, increased profits, and improved patient outcomes. This book aims to provide a comprehensive guide to drug sales forecasting.

Chapter 2: Basics of Drug Sales Forecasting

Drug sales forecasting involves estimating the demand for a particular drug in a given period. The forecasting process considers various factors that can affect demand, such as demographics, disease prevalence, competition, and market trends. The forecasting process can be qualitative or quantitative, depending on the data available and the forecast accuracy required.

Chapter 3: Qualitative Forecasting Methods

Qualitative forecasting methods rely on expert opinions, market research, and subjective assessments to predict sales. These methods are useful when there is limited historical data or when the market conditions are rapidly changing. Some qualitative forecasting methods include the Delphi method, market research, and expert opinions.

Chapter 4: Quantitative Forecasting Methods

Quantitative forecasting methods use historical data to predict future sales. These methods can be more accurate than qualitative methods, but they require extensive data analysis and statistical modeling. Some quantitative forecasting methods include time series analysis, regression analysis, and neural networks.

Chapter 5: Combining Qualitative and Quantitative Forecasting Methods

The best forecasting results can be achieved by combining qualitative and quantitative methods. Combining methods allows for a more comprehensive analysis of the market, taking into account both subjective and objective factors. This approach can improve forecast accuracy and lead to better business decisions.

Chapter 6: Challenges in Drug Sales Forecasting

Drug sales forecasting is not without its challenges. The market for drugs can be unpredictable, and demand can fluctuate based on various factors such as regulatory changes and unexpected events. There is also the challenge of forecasting for new drugs that do not have a historical sales record. Overcoming these challenges requires a flexible and adaptive approach to forecasting.

Chapter 7: Technology in Drug Sales Forecasting

Advances in technology have improved drug sales forecasting. Big data analytics, machine learning, and artificial intelligence are now used to analyze large datasets and make accurate predictions. These technologies can also help pharmaceutical companies identify new market opportunities and optimize their sales strategies.

Chapter 8: Case Studies

This chapter presents case studies of drug sales forecasting in action. The case studies demonstrate how different forecasting methods can be applied to different drugs and markets. The case studies also highlight the importance of accurate forecasting in achieving business objectives.

Chapter 9: Conclusion

Drug sales forecasting is a crucial aspect of pharmaceutical companies' operations. Accurate forecasting can lead to cost savings, increased profits, and improved patient outcomes. The forecasting process involves a combination of qualitative and quantitative methods, which can be challenging but rewarding. Advances in technology have improved the forecasting process, and pharmaceutical companies should continue to embrace new technologies to improve their forecasting accuracy.

Chapter 1: Introduction

Drug sales forecasting is an essential aspect of pharmaceutical companies' operations. In the pharmaceutical industry, sales forecasting refers to the process of predicting the future demand for a particular drug over a given period. Sales forecasting is crucial for pharmaceutical companies as it helps them plan for production, marketing, and distribution of their drugs. The process of forecasting sales involves analyzing historical data, market trends, and other factors that can affect demand.

Sales forecasting also plays a crucial role in financial planning and budgeting for pharmaceutical companies. Accurate sales forecasting can lead to cost savings, increased profits, and improved patient outcomes. By accurately forecasting sales, companies can optimize their resources and minimize waste. Sales forecasting also helps companies make informed decisions about pricing, promotion, and product development.

Pharmaceutical companies operate in a highly competitive environment, and accurate sales forecasting is crucial for gaining a competitive edge. Accurate forecasting can help companies identify new market opportunities, optimize their sales strategies, and make better-informed decisions. Inaccurate sales forecasting, on the other hand, can lead to excess inventory, lost sales, and missed opportunities.

The purpose of this book is to provide a comprehensive guide to drug sales forecasting. The book will cover the basics of drug sales forecasting, including the different methods used in the process. It will also cover the challenges associated with drug sales forecasting and how to overcome them. The book will highlight the role of technology in drug sales forecasting and present case studies to demonstrate how different forecasting methods can be applied in real-world situations.

In conclusion, drug sales forecasting is a critical aspect of pharmaceutical companies' operations. Accurate sales forecasting can lead to cost savings, increased profits, and improved patient outcomes. By providing a comprehensive guide to drug sales forecasting, this book aims to equip pharmaceutical companies with the knowledge and tools they need to make informed decisions and stay ahead of the competition.

Chapter 2: Basics of Drug Sales Forecasting

Drug sales forecasting is the process of estimating the demand for a particular drug in a given period. The forecasting process considers various factors that can affect demand, such as demographics, disease prevalence, competition, and market trends. The forecasting process can be qualitative or quantitative, depending on the data available and the forecast accuracy required.

Qualitative Forecasting Methods

Qualitative forecasting methods rely on expert opinions, market research, and subjective assessments to predict sales. These methods are useful when there is limited historical data or when the market conditions are rapidly changing. Some qualitative forecasting methods include the Delphi method, market research, and expert opinions.

The Delphi method is a forecasting technique that involves soliciting opinions from a panel of experts. The experts are asked to provide their estimates of future sales, and the results are compiled and analyzed. This method is useful when there is no historical data available or when the market conditions are rapidly changing.

Market research involves gathering data from customers, competitors, and other sources to predict sales. Market research can include surveys, focus groups, and interviews. This method is useful for understanding customer needs and preferences and identifying market opportunities.

Expert opinions are another source of qualitative data for drug sales forecasting. Experts in the field can provide insights into market trends, new therapies, and other factors that can affect demand.

Quantitative Forecasting Methods

Quantitative forecasting methods use historical data to predict future sales. These methods can be more accurate than qualitative methods, but they require extensive data analysis and statistical modeling. Some quantitative forecasting methods include time series analysis, regression analysis, and neural networks.

Time series analysis involves analyzing historical sales data to identify patterns and trends. This method is useful for forecasting sales for established drugs with a stable market.

Regression analysis involves identifying the relationship between sales and other factors such as price, advertising, and demographics. This method is useful for forecasting sales for new drugs with no historical data.

Neural networks are a type of artificial intelligence that can analyze large datasets and make predictions. This method is useful for forecasting sales for drugs with complex market dynamics.

Combining Qualitative and Quantitative Forecasting Methods

The best forecasting results can be achieved by combining qualitative and quantitative methods. Combining methods allows for a more comprehensive analysis of the market, taking into account both subjective and objective factors. This approach can improve forecast accuracy and lead to better business decisions.

In conclusion, drug sales forecasting involves estimating the demand for a particular drug in a given period. The forecasting process considers various factors that can affect demand, such as demographics, disease prevalence, competition, and market trends. The forecasting process can be qualitative or quantitative, depending on the data available and the forecast accuracy required. Combining qualitative and quantitative methods can lead to more accurate forecasts and better business decisions.

Chapter 3: Qualitative Forecasting Methods

Qualitative forecasting methods rely on expert opinions, market research, and subjective assessments to predict sales. These methods are useful when there is limited historical data or when the market conditions are rapidly changing. Qualitative forecasting methods are particularly useful for forecasting sales of new drugs where there is no historical data available.

The three main qualitative forecasting methods used in the pharmaceutical industry are the Delphi method, market research, and expert opinions.

Delphi Method

The Delphi method is a qualitative forecasting technique that involves soliciting opinions from a panel of experts. The experts are asked to provide their estimates of future sales, and the results are compiled and analyzed. The Delphi method is particularly useful when there is no historical data available or when the market conditions are rapidly changing.

The Delphi method is a multi-round process that involves several iterations of questionnaires and feedback. In the first round, the panel of experts is provided with information about the drug and the market. The experts are then asked to provide their estimates of future sales.

In the second round, the experts are provided with the estimates of the other experts and are asked to revise their estimates. This process is repeated until a consensus is reached.

Market Research

Market research involves gathering data from customers, competitors, and other sources to predict sales.

Market research can include surveys, focus groups, and interviews. Market research is particularly useful for understanding customer needs and preferences and identifying market opportunities.

Market research can provide valuable insights into customer preferences, price sensitivity, and brand perception. Market research can also provide information on the size and growth potential of the market.

Expert Opinions

Expert opinions are another source of qualitative data for drug sales forecasting. Experts in the field can provide insights into market trends, new therapies, and other factors that can affect demand. Experts can include clinicians, pharmacists, and industry professionals.

Expert opinions can be obtained through surveys, interviews, and focus groups. Expert opinions can provide valuable insights into the market, particularly for new drugs where there is limited historical data.

Advantages and Disadvantages of Qualitative Forecasting Methods

Qualitative forecasting methods have several advantages and disadvantages.

Advantages:

Qualitative methods can be used when there is limited historical data available.

Qualitative methods can be used when the market conditions are rapidly changing.

Qualitative methods can provide valuable insights into customer preferences and brand perception.

Qualitative methods can be used to identify market opportunities and trends.

Disadvantages:

Qualitative methods are subjective and may be biased.

Qualitative methods are dependent on the expertise of the participants.

Qualitative methods may not be as accurate as quantitative methods.

Qualitative methods can be time-consuming and expensive.

In conclusion, qualitative forecasting methods rely on expert opinions, market research, and subjective assessments to predict sales. Qualitative forecasting methods are particularly useful when there is limited historical data available or when the market conditions are rapidly changing. The three main qualitative forecasting methods used in the pharmaceutical industry are the Delphi method, market research, and expert opinions. Qualitative forecasting methods have several advantages and disadvantages, and the best results can be achieved by combining qualitative and quantitative methods.

Chapter 4: Quantitative Forecasting Methods

Quantitative forecasting methods use historical data to predict future sales. These methods can be more accurate than qualitative methods, but they require extensive data analysis and statistical modeling. Quantitative methods are particularly useful when there is a significant amount of historical data available.

The three main quantitative forecasting methods used in the pharmaceutical industry are time series analysis, regression analysis, and neural networks.

Time Series Analysis

Time series analysis involves analyzing historical sales data to identify patterns and trends. Time series analysis is particularly useful when the data exhibits seasonality or other recurring patterns.

Time series analysis involves four components: trend, seasonality, cyclical fluctuations, and random fluctuations. The trend component refers to the long-term direction of the data. The seasonality component refers to the periodic fluctuations in the data. The cyclical fluctuations refer to long-term fluctuations that are not seasonal. The random fluctuations refer to short-term fluctuations that are not predictable.

Regression Analysis

Regression analysis involves analyzing the relationship between the dependent variable (sales) and one or more independent variables (such as price, advertising, and promotion). Regression analysis is particularly useful for identifying the factors that drive sales.

Regression analysis involves estimating a mathematical equation that represents the relationship between the dependent variable and the independent variables. The equation can be used to predict future sales based on changes in the independent variables.

Neural Networks

Neural networks are a type of artificial intelligence that can be used to predict sales. Neural networks are particularly useful for analyzing complex data sets with multiple variables.

Neural networks work by simulating the function of the human brain. The network consists of layers of interconnected nodes (neurons) that process the input data. The output of the network is a prediction of future sales.

Advantages and Disadvantages of Quantitative Forecasting Methods

Quantitative forecasting methods have several advantages and disadvantages.

Advantages:

Quantitative methods can be more accurate than qualitative methods.

Quantitative methods can identify the factors that drive sales.

Quantitative methods can be used to forecast sales for multiple time periods.

Quantitative methods can be automated, saving time and resources.

Disadvantages:

Quantitative methods require extensive data analysis and statistical modeling.

Quantitative methods assume that the future will be similar to the past.

Quantitative methods can be influenced by outliers and data errors.

Quantitative methods may not capture all the factors that affect sales.

In conclusion, quantitative forecasting methods use historical data to predict future sales. The three main quantitative forecasting methods used in the pharmaceutical industry are time series analysis, regression analysis, and neural networks. Quantitative forecasting methods have several advantages and disadvantages, and the best results can be achieved by combining qualitative and quantitative methods.

Chapter 5: Combining Qualitative and Quantitative Forecasting Methods

The best forecasting results can be achieved by combining qualitative and quantitative methods. Combining methods allows for a more comprehensive analysis of the market, taking into account both subjective and objective factors. This approach can improve forecast accuracy and lead to better business decisions.

Combining Qualitative and Quantitative Methods

The process of combining qualitative and quantitative methods involves several steps:

Step 1: Identify the Key Drivers of Demand

The first step in combining methods is to identify the key drivers of demand.

These drivers can include demographic factors, disease prevalence, market trends, and competition.

Step 2: Use Qualitative Methods to Identify Market Trends

The second step is to use qualitative methods, such as expert opinions or market research, to identify market trends that are not captured by historical data. For example, an expert may have insights into a new competitor entering the market that is not yet reflected in historical sales data.

Step 3: Use Quantitative Methods to Analyze Historical Data

The third step is to use quantitative methods, such as time series analysis or regression analysis, to analyze historical data and identify the relationships between sales and the key drivers of demand.

Step 4: Combine Qualitative and Quantitative Results

The final step is to combine the results of the qualitative and quantitative analyses. This can involve adjusting the quantitative forecast based on the qualitative insights or vice versa. For example, if the quantitative forecast suggests strong sales growth but the qualitative analysis suggests a new competitor may impact sales, the final forecast may be adjusted downward to account for this.

Advantages of Combining Qualitative and Quantitative Methods

Combining qualitative and quantitative methods has several advantages:

Comprehensive Analysis: Combining methods allows for a more comprehensive analysis of the market, taking into account both subjective and objective factors.

Improved Forecast Accuracy: Combining methods can improve forecast accuracy by incorporating insights that are not captured by historical data.

Better Business Decisions: Improved forecast accuracy can lead to better business decisions, such as more effective production planning or more targeted marketing efforts.

More Robust Analysis: Combining methods can also make the analysis more robust by reducing the impact of outliers and data errors.

Disadvantages of Combining Qualitative and Quantitative Methods

There are also some potential disadvantages to combining qualitative and quantitative methods:

Time-Consuming: Combining methods can be time-consuming, requiring extensive data analysis and expert input.

Subjective Input: The qualitative input may be subjective and influenced by personal biases.

Additional Complexity: Combining methods can add additional complexity to the forecasting process, requiring specialized expertise in both qualitative and quantitative methods.

Conclusion

In conclusion, combining qualitative and quantitative methods can lead to more accurate and robust sales forecasts. The process involves identifying the key drivers of demand, using qualitative methods to identify market trends, using quantitative methods to analyze historical data, and combining the results. While there are potential disadvantages to this approach, the benefits of improved forecast accuracy and better business decisions make it a worthwhile strategy for pharmaceutical companies.

Chapter 6: Challenges in Drug Sales Forecasting

Drug sales forecasting is not without its challenges. The market for drugs can be unpredictable, and demand can fluctuate based on various factors such as regulatory changes and unexpected events. There is also the challenge of forecasting for new drugs that do not have a historical sales record. Overcoming these challenges requires a flexible and adaptive approach to forecasting.

Challenges in Drug Sales Forecasting

There are several challenges in drug sales forecasting:

Unpredictable Market: The market for drugs can be unpredictable, with demand fluctuating based on various factors such as regulatory changes, shifts in disease prevalence, or unexpected events such as a pandemic. These factors can make it difficult to accurately forecast sales.

New Drugs: Forecasting for new drugs that do not have a historical sales record is challenging. There may be limited data available to guide the forecasting process, and the market response to a new drug can be unpredictable.

Limited Data: Even for drugs with an established sales history, there may be limited data available. This can make it difficult to identify trends and patterns in sales data, which can impact the accuracy of forecasts.

Complex Market: The pharmaceutical market is complex, with multiple stakeholders and a constantly evolving landscape. Forecasting in this environment requires an understanding of the regulatory environment, healthcare policies, and market trends.

Competition: The competitive landscape in the pharmaceutical industry can also impact sales forecasts. New entrants into the market can impact demand for existing drugs, and competitive pricing pressures can impact revenue.

Overcoming Challenges in Drug Sales Forecasting

To overcome these challenges, pharmaceutical companies must adopt a flexible and adaptive approach to forecasting. This approach should involve:

Continuous Monitoring: The pharmaceutical market is constantly evolving, and forecasting should be an ongoing process. Continuous monitoring of market trends, regulatory changes, and disease prevalence can help companies stay ahead of the curve and adjust their forecasts as needed.

Collaboration: Collaboration between different departments within the company, such as marketing and research, can help ensure that forecasts are based on a comprehensive understanding of the market.

Data Analysis: Robust data analysis is essential for accurate forecasting. Companies should invest in tools and expertise to analyze sales data, identify trends, and make informed projections.

Scenario Planning: Scenario planning involves considering multiple potential outcomes and developing contingency plans based on each. This approach can help companies prepare for unexpected events and minimize the impact of market volatility.

Forecast Accuracy: Forecast accuracy should be regularly assessed and evaluated. Companies should consider using metrics such as Mean Absolute Percentage Error (MAPE) to measure the accuracy of their forecasts and identify areas for improvement.

Conclusion

Drug sales forecasting is not without its challenges, but companies can overcome these challenges through a flexible and adaptive approach to forecasting. This approach should involve continuous monitoring of the market, collaboration between departments, robust data analysis, scenario planning, and regular evaluation of forecast accuracy. By adopting these strategies, pharmaceutical companies can improve the accuracy of their sales forecasts and make better business decisions.

Chapter 7: Technology in Drug Sales Forecasting

Advances in technology have transformed the way drug sales

forecasting is performed. Big data analytics, machine learning, and artificial intelligence (AI) are now being used to analyze large datasets and make accurate predictions. These technologies have also helped pharmaceutical companies identify new market opportunities and optimize their sales strategies.

Big Data Analytics

The explosion of big data has created opportunities for pharmaceutical companies to gather and analyze vast amounts of data from various sources, including electronic medical records, social media, and clinical trials. Big data analytics allows companies to identify patterns, trends, and correlations that may not be immediately apparent through traditional analysis methods. By analyzing this data, companies can gain insights into market trends, patient behavior, and disease prevalence, which can be used to make accurate sales forecasts.

Machine Learning

Machine learning is a subset of AI that enables computer systems to learn from data without being explicitly programmed. Machine learning algorithms can analyze historical sales data and identify patterns and correlations that may not be immediately apparent to humans. These algorithms can also adapt and improve over time as new data becomes available. Machine learning can be used to predict sales trends, identify factors that impact sales, and optimize sales strategies.

Artificial Intelligence

AI is a broad term that encompasses machine learning, natural language processing, and other advanced technologies. AI can be used to analyze vast amounts of data, identify patterns and correlations, and make predictions. AI can also be used to automate routine tasks, freeing up resources for more strategic activities. AI can be used to optimize sales strategies, identify new market opportunities, and improve sales forecasts.

Benefits of Technology in Drug Sales Forecasting

The use of technology in drug sales forecasting offers several benefits:

Improved Accuracy: Technology can help improve the accuracy of sales forecasts by analyzing large datasets and identifying patterns and correlations that may not be immediately apparent through traditional analysis methods.

Faster Analysis: Technology can analyze large datasets in a fraction of the time it would take a human analyst. This enables companies to make more informed decisions quickly.

Better Insights: Technology can identify new market opportunities and optimize sales strategies based on data-driven insights.

Reduced Costs: Technology can automate routine tasks, freeing up resources for more strategic activities. This can lead to cost savings and increased productivity.

Challenges of Technology in Drug Sales Forecasting

While technology offers several benefits, there are also challenges to its adoption:

Data Quality: The accuracy of sales forecasts is only as good as the data that is used to generate them. Poor data quality can lead to inaccurate forecasts.

Data Privacy: The use of big data raises concerns about data privacy and security. Companies must ensure that they are collecting and using data in compliance with regulatory requirements and ethical standards.

Integration: Integrating new technology into existing systems can be challenging. Companies must ensure that new technology can integrate seamlessly with existing systems to avoid disruption.

Conclusion

Advances in technology have transformed drug sales forecasting, enabling companies to analyze large datasets, identify patterns, and make accurate predictions. Big data analytics, machine learning, and AI have all contributed to improved sales forecasting accuracy, faster analysis, better insights, and reduced costs. However, there are also challenges to the adoption of new technology, including data quality, data privacy, and integration. By addressing these challenges and leveraging the benefits of technology, pharmaceutical companies can improve their sales forecasting capabilities and make better business decisions.

Chapter 8: Case Studies

Drug sales forecasting is a critical aspect of the pharmaceutical industry, enabling companies to plan their production, marketing, and distribution strategies. Accurate forecasting can lead to cost savings, increased profits, and improved patient outcomes. In this chapter, we present case studies of drug sales forecasting in action, highlighting the different methods used and the benefits of accurate forecasting.

Case Study 1: Forecasting the Launch of a New Drug

In this case study, a pharmaceutical company is planning to launch a new drug to treat a specific medical condition. The company has limited historical data on the market and the disease, making traditional quantitative forecasting methods challenging. Therefore, the company decided to use a combination of qualitative and quantitative methods to forecast sales.

First, the company conducted market research to understand the disease's prevalence, the target patient population, and the competitive landscape. They also consulted with experts in the field to gain insights into the drug's efficacy and potential demand.

Next, the company used time-series analysis to forecast sales based on historical data for similar drugs and the disease's prevalence over time. They also used regression analysis to identify the factors that could impact sales, such as the drug's price, marketing spend, and physician adoption rate.

By combining qualitative and quantitative methods, the company was able to develop an accurate forecast for the drug's launch. The forecast allowed them to plan production, marketing, and distribution strategies, ensuring that they had the resources in place to meet demand.

Case Study 2: Forecasting Sales for an Established Drug

In this case study, a pharmaceutical company is looking to forecast sales for an established drug that has been on the market for several years. The drug treats a chronic condition, and the company has access to several years of sales data.

The company used time-series analysis to forecast sales for the upcoming year, taking into account seasonality, trend, and the drug's historical sales. They also used regression analysis to identify the factors that could impact sales, such as changes in the competitive landscape or regulatory changes.

To improve the accuracy of their forecast, the company incorporated machine learning techniques, such as decision trees and random forests. These techniques allowed them to analyze large datasets and identify the most critical variables impacting sales.

By using a combination of traditional and advanced forecasting methods, the company was able to develop an accurate forecast for the drug's sales. The forecast allowed them to optimize their marketing and distribution strategies, ensuring that they could meet demand while minimizing costs.

Case Study 3: Forecasting Sales in a Competitive Market

In this case study, a pharmaceutical company is competing in a crowded market with several similar drugs. The company has access to several years of sales data, but the market is rapidly changing, making traditional forecasting methods less effective.

To develop an accurate forecast, the company used a combination of quantitative and qualitative methods. They conducted market research to understand the competitive landscape and identify areas of opportunity. They also used time-series analysis to forecast sales based on historical data for similar drugs.

To account for the rapidly changing market, the company incorporated machine learning techniques, such as neural networks and deep learning. These techniques allowed them to analyze large datasets and identify patterns that would have been challenging to identify using traditional methods.

By using a combination of traditional and advanced forecasting methods, the company was able to develop an accurate forecast for the drug's sales. The forecast allowed them to optimize their marketing and distribution strategies, ensuring that they could compete effectively in a crowded market.

Conclusion

Drug sales forecasting is critical for pharmaceutical companies, enabling them to plan production, marketing, and distribution strategies. By using a combination of qualitative and quantitative methods, pharmaceutical companies can develop accurate forecasts that allow them to optimize their business strategies. The case studies presented in this chapter demonstrate the benefits of accurate forecasting and the importance of using flexible and adaptive

Chapter 9: Conclusion

In conclusion, drug sales forecasting is a critical aspect of pharmaceutical companies' operations. The ability to accurately predict the demand for a drug can have a significant impact on a company's financial performance and patient outcomes. Forecasting is a complex process that involves a combination of qualitative and quantitative methods.

Qualitative methods, such as expert opinions and market research, provide valuable insights into the market and patient needs. Quantitative methods, such as statistical models, use historical data to predict future sales. Combining these methods can result in more accurate forecasts.

The pharmaceutical industry has undergone significant changes in recent years. Advances in technology, such as big data analytics, artificial intelligence, and machine learning, have improved the forecasting process. These technologies enable pharmaceutical companies to analyze vast amounts of data quickly and accurately, resulting in more reliable forecasts.

Pharmaceutical companies should continue to embrace new technologies to improve their forecasting accuracy. However, it is essential to keep in mind that technology is not a substitute for human expertise. The forecasting process requires a combination of technology and human input to achieve the best results.

Accurate drug sales forecasting can lead to significant cost savings, increased profits, and improved patient outcomes. It enables pharmaceutical companies to optimize their manufacturing and supply chain operations and ensure that they have enough inventory to meet demand. In turn, this helps to avoid stockouts and drug shortages, which can have serious consequences for patient health.

In conclusion, drug sales forecasting is a challenging but rewarding process that is essential for the success of pharmaceutical companies. By embracing new technologies and combining qualitative and quantitative methods, pharmaceutical companies can improve their forecasting accuracy, reduce costs, and ultimately, improve patient outcomes.

Some cases on Drug Forecasting

Case Study 1: Utilizing Machine Learning for Drug Forecasting

Problem:

A pharmaceutical company was struggling with accurate sales forecasting for their newly developed drug targeting a niche market segment. Traditional methods were proving inadequate due to the complexity of the market dynamics and the limited historical data available.

Solution:

The company employed advanced machine learning techniques to forecast sales for their new drug. They gathered data from various sources including clinical trial results, patient demographics, competitor activities, and market trends. Using predictive modeling algorithms such as random forest and neural networks, they developed a sophisticated forecasting model capable of analyzing vast amounts of data and predicting future sales with higher accuracy.

Outcome:

By implementing machine learning for drug forecasting, the pharmaceutical company achieved significant improvements in sales predictions. The accurate forecasts helped them optimize inventory management, production planning, and marketing strategies. With better insights into future demand, the company reduced stockouts and excess inventory, leading to cost savings and increased revenue. Moreover, the ability to anticipate market trends enabled them to adapt quickly to changing dynamics, gaining a competitive edge in the industry.

Case Study 2: Incorporating Real-Time Data Analytics for Drug Sales Forecasting

Problem: A global pharmaceutical company faced challenges in forecasting sales for its portfolio of drugs due to the dynamic nature of the market and the influence of external factors such as regulatory changes and emerging competitor products. Traditional forecasting methods based on historical data alone were insufficient to capture these complexities.

Solution:

The company implemented a real-time data analytics platform that continuously monitored various factors influencing drug sales, including prescription trends, patient demographics, physician preferences, and market dynamics. By integrating advanced analytics techniques such as predictive modeling and sentiment analysis, they developed a dynamic forecasting system capable of adapting to changing market conditions in real-time.

Outcome:

The adoption of real-time data analytics revolutionized the company's approach to drug forecasting. The agile forecasting system provided timely insights into market trends, enabling proactive decision-making and rapid adjustments to sales strategies. As a result, the company achieved better accuracy in sales forecasts, reduced inventory holding costs, and improved overall operational efficiency. Additionally, the ability to anticipate market shifts allowed them to capitalize on emerging opportunities and mitigate risks effectively, driving sustainable growth in sales and market share.

Case Study 3: Collaborative Forecasting Approach for Drug Sales Prediction

Problem:

A mid-sized pharmaceutical company faced challenges in accurately forecasting sales for its diverse portfolio of drugs across different therapeutic areas. The existing forecasting process lacked integration between sales, marketing, and supply chain teams, leading to discrepancies and inefficiencies in demand planning.

Solution:

The company adopted a collaborative forecasting approach that involved cross-functional teams working together to leverage their collective expertise and insights. They implemented a collaborative forecasting platform that enabled seamless communication and data sharing between sales, marketing, and supply chain departments. Through regular meetings and workshops, stakeholders collaborated on developing consensus-based forecasts that incorporated inputs from various perspectives.

Outcome:

The collaborative forecasting approach resulted in more accurate and reliable sales predictions for the pharmaceutical company. By harnessing the collective intelligence of cross-functional teams, they were able to capture a holistic view of market dynamics and factors influencing demand. This led to improved alignment between sales forecasts and actual performance, reducing forecasting errors and improving inventory management efficiency. Moreover, the collaborative approach fostered greater transparency and communication across departments, facilitating faster decision-making and enhancing overall organizational agility. As a result, the company achieved better customer service levels, optimized resource allocation, and ultimately, increased profitability.

www.ingramcontent.com/pod-product-compliance
Lightning Source LLC
Chambersburg PA
CBHW070351230526
45471CB00006B/2514